AS IF A RAVEN

AS IF A RAVEN

Yvonne Blomer

Palimpsest Press
1171 Eastlawn Ave.
Windsor, Ontario. N8S 3J1
www.palimpsestpress.ca

Book and cover design by Dawn Kresan. Typeset in Minion Pro
and Bodoni. Printed offset on Rolland Zephyr Laid at Coach House
Printing in Ontario, Canada. Edited by Carmine Starnino.

Palimpsest Press would like to thank the Canada Council for the Arts,
and the Ontario Arts Council for their support of our publishing
program. We also acknowledge the assistance of the Government
of Ontario through the Ontario Book Publishing Tax Credit.

Library and Archives Canada Cataloguing in Publication

Blomer, Yvonne, author
As if a raven / Yvonne Blomer.

POEMS. ISBN 978-1-926794-19-8 (PBK.)

    I. TITLE.

PS8553.L5657A8 2014   C811'.6   C2013-908206-9

As if a Raven is dedicated to my parents
Clive and Rita Blomer

The Western religious regard for the world often seems to amount to an attention to the world that thrusts the world aside to grasp the presumed light within. It is a form of inadvertence; it is too composed; it is not quite credible; it looks wrong; it has no wildness in it.
—Tim Lilburn, *Living in The World As If It Were Home*

CONTENTS

Bird I say   11

                              15   The Idolatry of Raven

Recreation   16
Abstine   17
Vulnus   18
Eglise saint Vallery   19
Nebuchadnezzar
among the ruins of Babylon   20
Still Life with Black Bird
on Lilac Branch   21
Pigeons   22
God and the Cuckoo   23

                              25   As If A Raven

Rainbow Calling   26
Undoing   28
Jacob's Ladder   29
Birdhouse in the
Terebinth Tree of Moreh   30
The Ascension of Squacco Heron 31
The Book of Ostrich   32
Added Beauty   34
Have you been hunting
March Train from
Cambridge to Brandon   36
Our Father   37
The Bird out of Paradise   38
Audubon: still life   39
The Pheasant at the
Side of the Road   40

Night Visit to Galla Placidia   41

The Birds of Castillo de San Jose   42

At the Pizzeria la Fornera   43

Hypocrite   44

Roll Call to the Ark   46

51   Raven's Skein

The Songs of Songs

1. To watch over …   52

II. Between plaited tresses   53

III. My beloved …   54

Bird of Freedom   55

The Turtle Dove   57

Storks, Eastern Europe   64

To Quail   65

Quail in the Graves of Greed   66

The Crusades   68

71   But for food we die/ we do

One Raven   72

The Lord God Bird   74

Bird, I say

What I know is what I perceive: birds eclipsing the trees
in chirrup and husk-crack crash. What I think, is bird; I mean, each
separate and named one. Bird we say is It and God is He. So I say
we are simply us, who have named everything yet seem nameless;
so many under one.

Bird I say, and mean: Water Fowl, that is Grebe and Loon, Cormorant
(I love the Cormorant for it gets wet and we get wet and it must
shiver as we do and feel the chill of life too), Gull and Duck, Swan
and Tern (but when I say Duck I mean—Mallard, Wigeon, Teal et
al), Coot, Heron, Crane, and move from Water to Shore and how
can I know—well let me tell you—Shore Birds have longer limbs,
long pointy bills for digging in sand or grit along the shoreline (I
think we are jealous of such fine brute strength).

So, you see, here is a kind of list that I am devising as I go (note that
I is always I and only i through force of will). What I want is each
and every bird, those that are and were and if there was a *Genesis* as
in *The Bible*, though Myth and Fact often run parallel, they are not
equal. Anyway, if there was a Genesis, then Every Bird must come
up and be celebrated, seen, characterised, captured in wildness or
in full-colour on screen. If there wasn't, as sometimes I might say,
every bird is considered and counted anyway. They are characters
(don't you sense the character of the afore mentioned Cormorant,
though there are varieties of said bird—the Pelagic, Double-crested,
Brandt's, Anhinga, Olivaceous, Red Faced, Great) and in the name
lies the character. Pelagic must suffer the sniffles; a seaman adrift
upon the open waves. While the Imperial Shag suffers the multiplicity
of its name: Imperial, Blue-Eyed, King. Each one differentiated, it
seems, by name and the variation in colour of its gular.

Do you see, here, how easily I am sidetracked? My hope and wish, think of me, a small passerine, maybe even, dare I say it, a vagrant Penduline Tit, flit, flit. Can I say, and I think it may fit, I'll quote "Acrobatic on thin twigs; sociable when not breeding". Dare I suggest a parallel: twig to line and yes, it has been a productive time.

just the word tit encaptures (in raptures)
the titillating tincture
feather on tongue
the tickle
your wry shy smile suggests
when blue, or bearded, grey
how you can simply make my day.

Poem, Bird, Bible: Wild. There is my thesis, of sorts.

BEAUTY too. Each letter of the word a revelation: Bee-Eater, Eagle, Antwren, Umbrellabird, Tawny Owl, Yellowhammer, Bunting, Egret, Albatross, Uniform Crake, Treecreeper, Yungas Manakin, Bittern, Eider, Antpitta, Upland Goose, Turtle Dove, Yellowthroat, Blackbird, Eared Grebe, Auk, Undulated Antshrike, Thrush, Yemen Serin, Blackcap, Elegant Tern, Antvireo, Unicolored Jay, Tinamou, Yap Monarch.

The Idolatry of Raven

Midday in the fields,
in the basin of the continent,
shadow pecks at shaded grass,
shapes hollow morning songs.

Then one, wings spread,
sees how clouds are feathered: as fish scales,
as tree branches, leaves, as a last breath
so chooses a dying man and silhouettes him:
contoured, light; flight stayed on black quill cross.

Flapping those dark-night wings,

Raven

rises where man falls,
casts an un-winged shadow.

Recreation

Heat on the sunbaked earth,
on the bare shoulders
of this wild pack of boys.
No cigarettes, no girls to pitch stones at;
mud-puddle-bored they scoop and cast
dirt into five lumps:
robin, finch, plump serin, round quail, sparrow.

Mud hardens.
Boys stand, sticky behind knees
stamp blood to feet, clap hands
over bird-like shapes. Sudden chirping motif:
Jesus' hands knock together,
shimmer of dust dusting back to earth,
lures his dirt-sparrow to birth.

Abstine

for Colwyn

"and that the humble friars, like little birds, should possess nothing
in this world, but should cast all the care of their lives on the
providence of God." —From *Little Flowers of St. Francis of Assisi*

On the rock mound, go to the rocks;
and on the dry bed of earth, taste it;
seeds left to feed you,
Chukar, taste your name
let it melt, name yourself—
Chogka, Hag'l, Rock
Partridge, *Alectoris graeca*
cannibal that flesh, hear it.
Savour, as you do, you do,
savour the dry mouth, the hunger.
In the coloured bands, in the red-rimmed
eyes, the red feet, see yourself.
In the fledglings, now fleeing.
In the egg, and the cock,
in the brightness and beauty of melanin,
your black bright stripes, know it.
Here is beauty, and here you abstain from it.
Food piled around, little dark flush,
you will leave it. And you will leave it
etched to the wall in the church of St. Francis
you will pluck up your wings
you will rest, rest in the hand of that man
and he will blow breath into you
and you will flee it.

Vulnus

A slight blush rises over the breast,
the taut neck of *Pelecanus onocrotalus*,
feathers sleekly arrayed, bill a smear
of yellow paint that dabs itself off at the throat,
at the gulp of throat, in the shadow of pink-rimmed
indignant eye. Pelican: mother of glory,
guilt when those powerful wings nuzzle in—
something akin to haste, taste of sharp mother-lust
and chicks get flattened somehow. A flush of anger,
this in-ornate ornis lets head lean in, pressure
on her fish-full pouch, taste of slither-finned
pink blood, not pierced breast of myth,
but the season stains horny chest and chicks revive
on flesh and blood of another kind.

Eglise Saint Vallery

Varengville-sur Mer, France

Here stone laid on stone, glued with mortar-
strength of hard-honed bone and muscle,
a boat-builder-gone-roofer's roof,
artisan's stained-glass windows and in the eaves
bone-still tongue of swallow holds heat-
softened half-burnt candle; drops it.—
Not food, nor nest-timber, not hardened shell
of young, nor hope held for too long.
That lone swallow sneaks, squeaks through
half-timber doors, grasps another and another,
lets them melt and stick to each other
in the crook of gargoyle's shoulder, on the shell-like roof
the accident-bred bird kleptomaniac brings
soft white half-moons that none, not even this one, can see—
how sunlight slowly feathers shape.

Nebuchadnezzar among the ruins of Babylon

Anchor yourself
to that sharp-winged silhouette
blanking out the sun.

A coarse cry rings, a portent: in the sky
the machines' blades cut
air, their shape the filigree that was your crown; but now

humanity holds the rock that shatters
your clay feet. Man was made from dirt,
and to dirt returns what he made:

history in the face of this eager call;
the peregrine's profile
shadowing what has already come.

Still life with Blackbird on Lilac Branch

Listen to those blackbirds. Gods
of the slick sun. Their voices:
a thick rolling on the tongue.
Listen to them crinkle and croon,
call out the fields, the blue,
puffed-up blooms, the eccentricity
of humans. There is origin and orgasm
in that trill chortle. Heart ring
heart beat, the finger-picked song
of the body letting go, leaping to
something as thin, as thick as air.

Pigeons

O, small coo calling.
Wherever I am, am going

your voice, just
over the wall.
The first voice
God heard
and in it a reminder of something
he'd done, wanted doing—

so in the morning he started
and Adam left the pigeon

                              pipire

to name itself.

So common, its coo
recalls each place you've ever been.
Its soft red feet point
to something you know
you've forgotten or
just remembered again.

God and the Cuckoo

In amongst juniper heaths, thickets
of thorn, heather, gorse: nests.
The wind rustles, shatters silence
to serve itself. A hepatic cuckoo
mouths the elliptical 'o' of her young,
one by one. It is the seventh day:
rest stretched only by the pleasure-
bringing call of the cuckoo. Barred
stripes of black along the contour
of red-orange feathers veil her
amid thorns, as she drops each egg
into each warbler's nest, each blackbird's.
This brood parasite: on the fourteenth day
when the world is but a week old
a fledgling cuckoo shoulders
its surrogate brothers and sisters
up, over the wall of nest, down
feathers not enough to block the spike of scrub.
Ya-koop, the cuckoo in Palestine,
God its Esau: little brother opening his mouth,
calling each passing passerine to lure food,
feed from its smaller host.

As If A Raven

"At the end of forty days Noah opened the window of the ark which he
had made, and sent forth a raven" —*Genesis*

Something in the name Raven makes you think hot
dried   blood blackred
why would anyone trust this bird
to come back
and not flap its crooked wings
in the new wild earth
making mountains where none were and monsters

You want to hear its call
know that something in fact is out there
powerful enough   a totem to sky and rain and water
that could harness this bird and call it back
it calling you back
ravenravingravenous

Rainbow Calling

On the oiled wood
of that all-encompassing Ark,
the Ostrich and other birds of its kind—
large eyed/ long limbed/ flightless—
above them, the sky adrift on cloud: a rainbow
formed of feathers, something
more than refracted light or sudden burst of flight.

That multi-hued arch was hooked from branch of boat
on wing and claw from Sharp-shinned Hawk
to brightly-spun Parrot, *kah-hah, hah, hahing*
up past the heavy mast, arching out from it,
like a wind-tattered, multi-coloured spinnaker;
sprawl of constant syncopated thrum.

They were calling, on wind and wing,

calling the Dove; feather-location
(wing-song), drum beat hum.
They were calling the Dove back
from the feral sky, from the tilt of torrential
water tongue: the Tawny Owl, Rufus-tailed Jacamar,
the many strains of Woodpecker,

all forms of bird, named

but barely known: Smooth-billed Ani, Lesser
Yellowlegs, the Marbled Godwit and the Laughing
Kookaburra held their ferocious wing-wrapped arms,
a furious smoke signal to seize
the Dove's lost flight. She'd gone
and come home, and gone again,

met Raven in an olive tree. Raven,

black as God's flooding heart,
begged her to stay, but instead
she stayed her unquiet breath
grabbed at olive bud and branch
then faced that colourless ebbing,
that surging cloud and her own diminishing

to go back to salt and wood and sea.

The arch of that tangible bone and feather arc
flapped firm, the Parrot going to and fro.
She put on a Noah-tone and cackled for each
to hang from land-bird, to large and unclean
to Pipit and Tit and the littlest holding fast
to claw or wing or beak.

When the Sacred Kingfisher saw a flash

white wing on white,
the Falcon, stooping out of formation, fell in a swoop—
one hundred nautical miles in a pulse—
to catch the Dove's lost last wind-ruptured spin.
The Hummingbirds hovered   feeding on fear
while the Dove, held on tender-hooks, stilled
in Falcon's grasp, stirred when released to the Ark at last.

The stratus thinned to reveal something not long seen:
sun slipping through cloud
cast some fragile light
on a bruised greenish-brown leaf
circling and circling in the wind and whirl
of wing: the many-hearted arc
held the sky up, as the one olive leaf fell.

Undoing

"Then the Lord said to Satan, 'So be it. He is in your hands;
but spare his life.'" —*Job* 2:6-7

The canal-centered Cormorant, suspended there,
and just now buoyant on some pogo-like stick—

the black sorrow of it
whose wings have de-evolved to scales.

It is like the nightmare: cells breaking back up,
tissue making air of itself.

The plump stone staying, nonetheless,
and quiet in your belly;

back arching, the weight of stone,
the undoing. It perches:

feathers become nails or scales of flaking
skin and the fowl falls in: cold

that womb of water
cold the old amphibian blood, and thin.

Jacob's Ladder

"…and he dreamed, and behold a ladder set up on the earth, and the top of it reached to heaven: and behold the angels of God ascending and descending on it." —*Genesis* 28:12

When that son of sons of fathers' dreams dreamt
he heard the loud crackle: feather on feather on
ozone on dream, fear followed on what could be cold
breath of fowl: not angels but the fidget of Cormorant
wings set out on rungs to dry in sun. Perched on faith
that big-footed water fowl got off-course somehow. Jacob,
going all nerves and nervous, saw angels' wings, saw stone
pillow as something of a temple, so oiled it, aiding the bird
so its feathered wings could bead water, let muggy air glide
off in its every direction. Double-crested, strange-billed, floppy-footed:
oaud oaud it alleged, beak on the bearing of hills, of still water.

Birdhouse in the Terebinth-tree of Moreh

When the Yellow Bellied Sapsucker was named
it threw its head back, let sap flow down, soft the
tube of throat, then tapped at pits on a narrowly-
focused horizon: the bleed of juice from the terebinth tree.

This temple will have dimensions fit to suspend:
inside the span of floor will be the length and breadth
of a woman's hand; its height the length of a man's foot. Outside
this tree-temple will cascade on wind, a waterfall: sound on shape.

A Master Craftsman, the Yellow Bellied Sapsucker is the envy
of the sugar hungry. Suspended amid branches
it pecks out, in perfect miniature squares, a way in.
This Ziggurat temple all wood, all nest of splendor.

Father-figure Sapsucker holds out insects, syrup-dipped,
to the hungry mouths of chicks. Beholden are the lesser
birds: hunger draws them to this chosen tree. Beholden
is man, lingering in shadow when the raucous voice calls.

The Ascension of Squacco Heron

Vagrant dewdrop drips
along elongated head feathers
as wings press air. A great quiet
thudding, trickle of marshy feet
rising up out of reeds.
There in the space between—
breath and sigh; sunlight
and fire: transcendence in flight:
tawny-orange goes sudden-white
and beyond shallow water, nothing
but sky, and sky, and this
crested bird's rough calling cry.

The Book of Ostrich

I.

"Which leaves her eggs in the earth, and warms them in dust.
And forgets that the foot may crush them or that the wild
beast may break them." —*Book of Job* 39:14-15

In the beginning there was dry brush, a horizon of
swelter gone light mist, shades of ostrich-white, dust.
The nomadic were drifting, sun catching on pink thighs,
wind tempering obdurate *bark* until it wafted out; quiet thump.
There was an egg and those nomads: males, females; omnivorous
omniscient male sat on shallow nest, scientific fact: in a moment of fea
let's say a nomad of another kind came by, yes on two legs, yes
thighs pinkening, lashes akin to these, their own;
but this one, male, is slow, diminished somehow, a threat
nonetheless; it comes down to the flight
or fight mentality: not all winged can fly so the first lays low so
large frame becomes mirage, bump in landscape:
egg nestled under the broad base of papa's rump,
his long neck curled round, head pressed down,
eyes held to what's behind him.

II.

"She is hardened against her young ones, as though they were
not hers… because God has deprived her of wisdom…"
—*The Book of Job 39:16-17*

Meanwhile, precocial chicks let long legs lift
ready to run desert sand through still soft toes
while dominant mom cluck-growls; chicks elude,
become seasonal shadow-bumps; then sand-sifting wallop
as male booms his shifting pleasure and female tucks down to dune.

III.

The Ostrich, the Israelites

how can any omniscient tell
if it made man from dust
or if it shaped an egg
and from it something winged
yet flightless fell

Added Beauty

after *Darwin and peacock lore*

yee-ow   yee-ow   yee-ow

To my untrained ear, longing. A creature more green, blue, under-feathers orange than any Kimono-clad or 18th century dandy in riding gear.

What I hear—wind in grass, insects, chirping passerines and in the distance, constant coo of dove—sets me on a quiet road in Southeast Asia, recalls the clack and click of tire tread and gears, bicycle pulling my shadow like a many-eyed tail.

The peacock carries everything on his back: train sweeps and marks his path, fan shades the blue-green neck and white-striped face, and the eyes, the eyes, the eyes.

What do you want out of life? More than vanity, by which I mean: fleeting breath, mist, the devil in its cry and Christ in its flesh; want more than this. All the way to Solomon who brought them to Israel; to Islamic lore where the pea-hen led Satan to the Garden of Eden.

My untrained ear is longing for this creature, more green, blue, under-feathers orange. The peacock carries everything on his back: train sweeps and marks his path, fan vibrates.

Perched on a branch now, on a leafless skeleton of tree, posing there, I think, orhow wind lifts the tail, eases the pressure somewhere between the wings. Lower back pain I might say, bicycle and road conveying me to a town which is a long afternoon away.

Wild bird, I wait all afternoon to see you fly with that *yee-ow, yee-ow*. Added beauty. My helmet is purple, it does nothing for me.

Have you been hunting?

after Brueghel II's *Christ in the house of Martha and Mary*, 1628

Christ, there are twelve birds at your unwashed feet, there
in the shadow of your glowing face, each much finer
than any one over the other:
a great spotted woodpecker, one magpie, but why?
two red-breasted warblers, two sparrows separated
by yellow-bellied, by gold-chested, something blue,
something used, some things dead and die and in beauty lie
at you, like-new. Oh those women, how they want you,
look at the tremor of breast, their long-longing gaze. Oh how you
fulfill all the expectations of time: puncture the lives
that would have thrilled those, your pallid eyes.

Have you been hunting, lord,
of earth of sea and sky? Why
feast and feed on that which could lift you, eye as breath
to soul, up beyond what seems whole, divine?
Have you been hunting, lord:
in the shadow of the door: fine plumage of peacock's tail, peacock
being pecked and picked for your feast? Flesh likened to your flesh.
How will you now decorate the skies: with opulent feathers,
some fine skull hollow in beauty as beauty in life?

March train from Cambridge to Brandon

"...some seed fell along the footpath and the birds came and ate it up."
—*Matthew* 13:3-8

Birds: scattered
over newly ploughed fields
are farmers, their hats off,
surveying their work;
are women, bandanas
holding back stray hairs,
picking latent berries,
digging for worms;
are pheasants, the sun reddening them;
are blackbirds growing blacker in the shadows;
are calling each other's call,
cracking husks
off each newly sown seed.

Our Father

Here, father, there is no heaven
hankered to your dreams.
The sparrows' song, the wrens'
are all; to earth they come, they call.
Relinquish this day of prayer, take bread,
tiptoe those long worn paths,
cast crumbs, whistle
and raise your hands to tree-tops.
The tawny feathered, the golden,
turquoise, grey and brown—
they flit, old man, they flit
and blow your dreams
with amens of song.

The bird
out of paradise

Early afternoon sun and me dawdling
like a cormorant, my flesh laid out to dry,
mind resort-ambiance-numb, and above
jet stream gone to wisps, blue sky
and stuck on it some black pterodactyl-winged
which makes me think: against these white stone walls
pre-history whisking like a vulture 'round
southern turret of this hotel,
which is some *Anime* dream.

The bird, perhaps a sea bird,
a dark angel, an omen or simple reminder:
look east: Mexico is out *there*
in the other world, the difficult one I want
to enter—like Eve on biting—
where no one cleans the streets
and hunger pangs at our gluttony.

Audubon: still life

"…his technique consisted of shooting as many birds of the same species as possible so that he could use them as models for his life size paintings." —*Everglades Digital Library*

What was nest has been skimmed
for bone structure, feather lustre,
feathers, beaks, fine-boned wings;
things that have gone missing from trees.
Children will not scream, will study
the pretty birds unflown,
not feasted on by fox or hound, no;
consumed by eye, finger, palette and brush.

To capture with rigour, death

consumed by eye, finger, palette and brush,
not feasted on by fox or hound, no;
the pretty birds unflown.
Children will not scream, will study
things that have gone missing from trees:
feathers, beaks, fine-boned wings,
for bone structure, feather lustre.
What was nest has been skimmed.

The Pheasant at the Side of the Road

This country is contoured, ripples
with the winding of paved roads, of hedgerows,
cattle grazing and sheep gone chill in fleecy opacity;
blackbirds pecking at just sown seeds, the whatever
they are that fly up between stalls of cows to startle
the morning, the moonlight; pheasants in their odd
beauty, their long trains, forgotten encumbrances.
In this pastoral field comes furtive speed of human glee
cruising narrow alleys, radio tuned, turned so loud
shrill flecks of bird fly off, rabbits run directionless,
sometimes off-beam.
What's passing us
when we build a world within a world: leave
such a car-cruising vastness; shadow of life in our slip-stream.

Night Visit to Galla Placidia

Ravenna, Italy

The four arches where doves bend to drink;
the four arches where doves perch ready to fly.

To live in these two worlds:
whether held to earth and all it demands, or to flight.

Outside, darkness wrapped in summer's heat.
My back to cold tile, my body wants to enter the water

of birth, of deer and bird; to enter the flicker of stars
even in this quiet place. No stirring, no sound. These doves

formed for contemplation; held, wing-tucked and bowed.
And my new son in dream; darkness, the puzzle

these tesserae form; images in coloured tile
mortared and mortared and mortared and only from a distance

something larger than the fragments. Held.
I hold my breath, I breathe. This lunar light, this

shattering of image by tile; building of image from tile.
moonlight serves it well, so well I want to believe.

The Birds of Castillo de San Jose

Lanzarote, Spain

Swallows sweep,
wing feathers brush
cliff edge, round turret
of lookouts over the reservoir
of Embalse de Guadalest.
On each sweep they reach higher,
higher, pass the stations
of the cross—
IX—as Christ falls, the birds rise;
X—He is stripped,
the swallows lose wind, still on air for a breath;
XI—Christ is nailed where
an earthquake shattered the gravestone
of Orduña; where the clatter
of high-top church bell
rings off each quarter
hour of the constant song
of swallow chasing song on wind
'round and 'round this hilltop;
history settling as old stone,
as voices hushed for listening.

At the Pizzeria la Fornera

for Rupert, Alicante, Spain

Not moonlight, nor sunlight, but day falls
partly candle-lit in this cave, this bodega
of restaurants that begins its turn toward dark.
At the round table for two
the Dutch couple, burnt red, becomes scraggly
Vultures, noses, beaks, sniff the tonic
that air is. The Spanish family of three chirps,
skirts under, flits to table edge, all Swallows
pecking at focaccia, dried thyme,
rosemary caught in the daughter's sliver of beak.
A German family and Spanish couple—
old friends or once-cousins become
two Magpies dining with the constant echo
of four Mocking Birds trying to learn something
of language. You and I sip Sangria, slip
a Loons long breathy song, watch and eat and get lost
in this rising mist of song.

Hypocrite

"The Lord said to Satan "Where have you come from?" Satan answered the Lord, "From going to and fro in the earth, and from walking up and down in it." The Lord said to Satan, "Have you considered my servant Job"" —*Job* 1:7-8

I.

The way he glides
one black foot loose
fanning at water
while the other leg kicks back
tucks in to rest on wing.
A saunter, a snap
solid orange beak trap.

Mute be the cob
but for his occasional hiss,
his quiet thoughtfulness,
for the lather-flap
of those lost-in-cloud wings.
They startle all the small things
they *humthrob*,
jolt the morning light.

II.

In a park, on a riverside walk:
hand holding (sunlight) crocus, lily,
long feather of *Cygnus Olor*
where colour is the absence of—
is white down on black skin;
puff of hiding-in
so they are not what they seem.

III.

One day the heavenly beings came
face in all that cloud and radiance
blinded by the corona of
shadow in embrace of
feathery white. What skin is so well hidden?
Ah Lord, have you considered
your servant Job
and how you drew that shadow self toward
fine brush strokes, the delight
of discourse? How one leg can rest
the other kick a firm swish stroke
to lead you where you go
to and fro.

The Roll Call to the Ark

                              Was it that He said a pair
was it that He said seven pairs
                              If it was a pair
if it was seven pairs
                              Then what of those un-hatched
what of those fledglings
                              What of inbreeding
souls and souls of silent sameness
                              If it was a pair
if it was seven pairs
                              Then let's start here
start with the lesser tit, the bearded
                              With the Golden Eagle, the Imperial
does He care how they are named
                              Does He care if they are beautiful
He does
                              They are
the sparrow
                              The Griffon Vulture
the golden oriole
                              The Peregrine
do you think He'd like how they look
                              So proud, such long thin necks
so small, such plumage
                              The Hoopoe, The Snow
finch, the skylark
                              Did His friend gather

the eggs of the robin, the dove
                    Crow, Raven eggs
did he eat any of them
                    Did he crack them over a fire
feed them to his sons
                    Feed them to his sons' wives
and how did he house them
                    In the ribs of a cypress
in an aviary of dream
                    For the Little Owl
for the tree pipit
                    Did he take the seeds of trees
did he take branches
                    Foliage
some arching trunk
                    Was it crowded with still eyes
was it loud with tweets and twitters and tittering
                    Did the sons
did the wives
                    Threaten to hunt
yell out amid eternal headaches
                    How
how
                    Did they gather
that small-winged
                    Those sharp-clawed
the goldcrest
                    The Fisher-Owl
and what did they eat
                    Did he build a lake

did he build a forest
                    Did he let them out
did they feed on fruit
                    Clean the flooded lands
clean the fly-laden tables
                    Of the ripening flesh
of the overripe rinds and cores
                    Did He ponder
did He consider
                    The length and breadth
the tiny-ness
                    Of The Harpy Eagle
the bee humming bird
                    Its taller-than-man wing span
its eggs smaller than the smallest finger nail
                    Its potential to catch up
its potential to hide
                    Did He consider
did He ponder
                    Hand-sized talons
all the tiny hiding places
                    Claws the length of a grizzly's
the arctic tern's yearly flight around the world?

Raven's Skein

"for love is but a skein unwound/ between the dark and dawn,"—Yeats

All night stars. Tenebrous, the switch forgotten. All night
as if a black skein, feathered, has been drawn.

Over the house three hard wires tightly wound.
Currents, measured in amps, power these small beams.

When Raven scooped the still water
and put out earth's fires, where was energy stored?

All night, wires grid the sloppy mismatched streets;
north to south, west and east, radial branches reach and reach.

The wet world, a clock radio tuned to static.
(perfect place for cranes)

All night stars, and Raven dampens them out.

By the light of a lamp, linked by a cable to a wall junction
to the cross-wires from house to house, this twisted skein.

We alight below the cloud line.

The Songs of Songs

I.

To watch over the vineyards

O carrion crow, pulpy skull of scarecrow
going soft in your black bill,
in this fetish-orange field lies worship:
the sweep of glossed plumage over glistening
membrane; lies the sweet blood of purple skinned grape
cut on your sharp edged tomia,
shimmering there: sun-light on wet earth.
You too sweet to ripe; you black in the shadows,
calling when you're calling—
the herds fly in dust gone crow, gone scare,
gone trill in clicks and shouts of *krrrkrrr.*

II.

Between plaited tresses
    Yellowhammer

If he were man, if she were as beautiful as he,
if she were man she'd ask: what is it you hide
under those gold and auburn plaited tresses
covering your chest, feathers full of carotenoids.
But she is bird, but he is bird and she is colour
blind to this beauty, but her ears are inside-out
fountains that let sound drip in, roll,
can you feel it roll now, that final
drawn-out rising and falling and calling
zizizizizziziie-diuh. What he hides, what she hears
is heartbeat, is breast bone letting syrinx fall,
is to man the place where collar bones meet,
the scooped out spot where a woman's pulse imitates the soft
vibration of a bird's wing ready for flight's take off.

III.

"My beloved is a cluster of henna blossom from the vineyards
of En-gedi" —*Song of Songs* 1:14

Beloved the bird's
sharp flute sound—*Sylvia atricapilla*
twittering at the edge
of this oasis, up from the salt-rich
shore of the Dead Sea at The Spring of the Goat,
ibex hairs caught as the hairs of a lover
webbed in underbrush, low
enough to soften the beds
of the Blackcap nesting in scrub,
those red-ringed
eyes among red berries,
the fragrance of love—
whistling its phrase gone cry;
the flight of birds startles
vines' silent quiver.

Bird of Freedom

"I am like a pelican of the wilderness: I am like an owl of the desert
I watch, and am as a sparrow alone upon the house top."
        —*Psalms* 102:6-7

Open palm, fingers the
barbs of the rachis,
hollow forms.

here

Pelican in the open
sea: wild
wilderness an unlocked gullet.

here

Open wing—
feathers shift in muscle:
dead appendage.

here I

Owl of the waste
places: silent as slipped on
aureole lighting some night sky.

I am

Finger to nail:
skein that holds blood in,
vane of wing.

here

Kos: little screeching
voice of feathers, plucked;
tear of umbilicus.

I am

Empty house: *hooklet*
of sparrow voice, refusing
to break: *tzippor deror.*

The Turtle Dove

after The Song of Songs

I.

Groom:

The song of turtle dove, the palest love;
this soft, this petticoat of feathers fine,
oh shaped of clay in breeze, oh you of every;
the wind is up, the day; this sun, what's left.
Cut, cut, cut this slip of will, this wind
of wind. Still that tumultuous heart,
this cool the colour dull as day, as light,
as down; this soft as feathers going dust.
In you the shadow: sun on sculpted seraph;
an angel's breath, something so wordless. Come
you dove of heart, you beauty—in this feathered
a heart flutters; a cry on wind:
oh turtle dove, oh brooding, oh nesting,
in this, my heart, the beat of all is cresting.

II.
Bride:

In this, my heart, the beat of all is cresting;
there is no stop, no resting. Cry of dove,
the feather rustle, muscle, bone of wish,
this laced on frame as light as air, as song
that twitches from an open wisp of chest;
in me this slimmer dove, that shaken core,
that you, this all: in longing breath, in song
in purring *tirrr*, in answering rustle, fall.
My love's left wing, this dove's all chill and shake;
here warmth, here smallest head on brightest wing:
this warming cup, that in need of. Bodies' heat,
oh breath's quick intake: round me contour's quill
all formed to shape. Oh timid as the dove
is timid: turtle heart, oh fragile love.

III.
Groom:

Is timid turtle heart, this fragile love,
as delicate: a robin's soft-blown egg?
My only sleeps, her lift and rest of chest,
a shimmer's gust of breath; is watched by bees,
the drunken swirl of flies, the lazy now
of ladybugs, of moths and harried wasps,
of spiders arching air into their webs.
This quiet breath on bill and bone in tongue:
of light, of summer's coming. Air is rich
with care: some god; this pant of wind it holds
her little all, this shiver, this too small.
My entire need: her shelter—from what?
Some force of dreams? Some scent of one who strays
in sleep, radiant wings a flutter of nerves.

IV.
Bride:

In sleep, radiant wings a flutter of nerves
awake now. Hark! the call of sharp in wing,
the coo of cliché bird, of feathers grey,
of bird too small to grow or menace prey.
But to that coo I rise, rise up to spring,
to rain's sweet end. To sun and silhouette,
to birds in song: to collared, stock to song
of turtle dove. He calls to me, he calls
the rains, the water's fountain; solid call
the sun to being, sweetest solid earth
he calls my heart, he sings this body's birth.
He rubs his feathers clean on green, on green.
He slices beak through brightest reeds, through tufts
of blossom: fruit of figs that sweetly bleed.

V.
Groom:

Of blossom: fruit of figs that sweetly bleed,
all wet on tongue, all liquid, all gone
to pomegranate seed: small eggs, such juice,
such fearless colour; full, my timid love
hides, burrows, digs heels in dirt,
a scurrying under that can only
hurt. In hiding, she's lying low.
Is she open, is she drawn to these
barbules, guarded shadows? What she hides,
a bride she is not, my pride

                                sick in heart
in heat, of dove-love this fragile shot-hard
heart. Oh heated pant, this driving good-god.
My passion pools: too old, too fooled. I flit
and flit, and flit up over springs of cool.

VI.
Bride:

and flit, and flit up over springs of cool
you small, you lost, you fool.

This fountain: me in bloom,
your garden: doom of doom.

I trill, I catch my voice
this fountain ear of ear

you hear, so fly to free
your heart, that flutter thing.

To tremble, shiver, cry—
I fly to nest, there's death

of hatchlings, my all, gone.
Oh sick in heart, go

to carrion, to crow.
my mirth will grow.

VII.
Groom:

My mirth will grow
my perfect one.
Your mirth my all—
a call of dove
a lasting smirk.
Beloved my
hot heart is hurt.
This pallid chest,
a beast in flight,
that breast of beat,
this not in me.
The song of you
sweet turtle dove
the palest love.

Storks, Eastern Europe

"Wednesday, 4 August. This morning, a small child who was playing in the sand was discovered at the pit. No one even tried to find out where he was from; they just shot him." —Witness, 1941, Museum at Paneriai

Agape   the stark bird
carnal its lust for worm

> If I could   as strong a beak
> in the shadow of stones

Chapel roof   white clutch   slender foot
taps on wires between concrete pylons

> Wilno   I say   my voice a soft squeak
> and the German woman understands where I have been—

café   open field   Baltic sea
Black-tailed stork steals

> Abattoir   the charnel house she says   Power lines
> Paneriai   I counter—
> black feather   pall

Nests   immense above muster of headstones
storks—awe ash rot

> a boy playing in the sand
> currant moon   portent these broods

What I have seen—storks on the wires
our ochre mouths hollow graves

To Quail

Exodus 16:13

And what of manna—some kind of joke,
the quail dropping, barely held by air,
pterylae in stunning browns, their ruffled
columns of fear. Plump for picking, and picked
they were, and like manna by morning
were they too nothing but maggots,
the stink of living, of waste, life's daily loss?

Quail in the Graves of Greed

Numbers 11:31

Tir tir tir

all day, after these last years of hunger, of
going without meat, the men and women quail,
heavy with their need.

Pick-per-vick

as if the second dove had found a forest
and in it the quail called back;
the coo of the dove being answered by some
flock of fat birds—fattened over spring
by something akin to husbandry. In the wind
that day, their flight held down for easy catching—
parallel to throwing the baby
with the bath water—why
not send them in the first place
rather than poison their fine flesh
to punish the greed that hunger for meat had brought?

Khau-vah

          quip-ip

His whispered call

          her short intake of breath.

If he shows himself in his voice

          he'll note it in hers

ruffle and thicken the breast plate
fly into the nets, mute.

quip-ip

she wants an answer to her call
but silently
she calls back
to silence.

this place is renamed Kibroth-hata'avah
a reminder to the Israelites how plague
can come to them too.

this place is renamed *Khau-tri-tir-pique-ip*
a reminder to the dumpy game bird
though their ears are hidden
they listen with the animal's loss,
their song echoing that of the dove's.

The Crusades

"That this foul deed shall smell above the earth
With carrion men, groaning for burial." —Shakespeare

After death all that is
is absent,
is carrion death.

All is a swarm of red kite
swooping and reeling, screeching out
to each bird of prey to *carry on, carry on:*

Imperial eagle, lammergeyer, the weight of what is,
a husbandry in the talons of Egyptian
vulture, griffon, condor

dig feet, their beaks in, and feed.

But for food we die/ we do

"Who provideth for the raven his food? When his young ones cry unto God, they wander for lack of meat." —*Book of Job 38:41*

                              The scraps   the seeds
                    don't mock   this   trick-
ster   ventriloquial   hard won   corvid

                                                            glossed
          blue-black   this knack for food foraging
                                    for finding the needle
                                              in the hay
                                    krok kroa kark

                    To prove this particular thorny point
        the one where hunger is hunger that ought to be settled by
                a hunter's hungry (searching) heart/need/want

So   Job   God and Raven walked into a forest for forty days
                God   using the *Corvus Corax* to prove his   bore-
                                              axe his point

        watch it   watch it   watch it
                                    oh Capital No-Man Man
        the power-full bill of this   blue-black   Raven
            is watching with his yellow-black-yellowbacked eyes

                              Krok Kroa Kark
                hark back Old Bearded Grey-Back (-ed GOD)
                        Raven's at your back.

One Raven (or that snag that makes a god of story)

shadow on bough
beak speaks   shape
earth in cloud

spear of light
on   charcoal-brittle-bird-muzzle

eye blinks
          ambit
       blanks out

black-beaked gargoyle
 black as being
          before light

 damp-winged on a wire
                    black when night calls

marionette-stringed
        shifting weather
                vane

flush with colour   silent prairie winter

chimera of light
        flight

black (with a little red in it) cloud rises where light falls

quill stiff as feathered wind
           as fish bone
                charcoal

scruffy coppered Raven thing
        stark as a city's lost sky

as a god('s) damned dark heart

The Lord God Bird

Forest path to river
on the way to river
bird song wild as sky.
Dog dogging to and
fallen trees stormed
to ground: all things
live and die.

-ba-Dam
as big as a spaniel, bigger, bold
blackred plumage;
bill that Elephant-
husk gleams. Audubon
Hero gathered whole treetops,
nesting family   to paint   vibrant
one perfection
as if reflection could be seen
captured.

Trickle of creek
lapping sound—
feral as skunk weed,
bright yellow, green
as my need to name,
make each thing I see.
Is the wild free—
to forage, yes, but tied
to that need. These birds
I write to place them back in the world.
Trap them instead
further into the making of—
wild as water
no longer creek bound
lapping, carelessly, at everything.

Pterodactyl-like. Old *Ivory Billed*—
some man stands in a tree
shadow, watches:
that bill peel, no, rip the skin off tree
in search of insects to feed on.
ba-DAM, be damned
if you will; you will be.

❀

Everything is larger than me. Dog wagging and bird chirping, in each I've taken to interpreting one for something human; in human is god, not in animal or plant or seed.

❀

If a tree falls… or to deepen
the cup—if a bird, *Good God*
don't. Bird, be bird
in the mossy morasses of forest.

❀

Each word alludes
to something in us.

Oh small singing bird
I cannot see you. In the end
all is an aviary and in it
I become "a bird of deep forest"

The stick, tick *(Lord-God)* trick
of naming: *Campephilus Principalis*
of the family Picidae—
because of their toes, their toes
of the Piciformes, class Aves
phylum Chordata—spinal
nerve and hollow-formed
Animalia, of course.
KA-BLACK!

Ah belief.

Oh *Campephilus Principalis:*
"principal lover of caterpillars"

Bill: bone, sheath of keratin,
broad at the base and deeply rooted.
Rooted in forage, held.
Released in air seized on wing.
These period pieces, red on white and black;
antiques of flesh and feather form.

In the act of believing, or of not;
believing rules over seeing, or feeling.
In the act of arguing
against, in the act of putting word to untamed
I trap (myself), clip the wings,
bonsai everything to fit this elegant glazed pot.

Principalis
First Among All.

This grandiose woodpecker
sometimes called: *the Van Dyck, White-black,*
Pate, Poule de bois, Kent, Tit-ka
is all, but, mostly, plucked and painted, gone.
But when seen: arrow-like shape, flag-span wings
ripping through forest canopy, language lost shape.
"The great bird cleaved its visage onto the eye of the seeing."

What is it, this—there is not a word for a thing existing
because a word is there to name it.

In all this metaphor   perhaps
their wildness   goes

               forgotten

Thrush as example of—

how I mull.

Notes to Poems

The opening epigraph is from Tim Lilburn, *Living in the World As If It Were Home.* Toronto: Cormorant Books, 2002. p. 42.

Bird I say: the quote starting "Acrobatic on thin twigs…" comes from J. Nicolai, D. Singer and K. Wothe. *Birds of Britain and Europe,* Trans and adapted by Ian Dawson. London: Collins Nature Guides, HarperCollins Publishers, 1993.

Recreation: the idea for this poem come from John Priestman's *God's Birds.* London: Burns and Oats, 1893.

Abstine: is inspired by a wall sculpture in the Basilica de San Francesco, Ravenna, Italy called *Patere/Abstine* to Endure/Abstain.

Vulnus: is after a cloister roof boss in Norwich Cathedral and subsequently seen in every church afterward as a wall sculpture of the pelican vulning itself to feed its young.

Nebuchadnezzar among the Ruins of Babylon: is after "Babylon: Cultural Vandalism." *The Guardian Newspaper,* January 15, 2005. Web.

Rainbow Calling: is inspired by the midrashim on Noah's Ark.

Jacob's Ladder: is inspired by the quote that is the poem's epigraph and also by the Jacob's ladder that is "a device for producing a continuous train of large sparks that rise upwards (named for the ladder to heaven)" from "Spark Gap: Visual Entertainment". Wikipedia.org. January 21, 2014. Web.

Birdhouse in the Terebinth-Tree of Moreh: comes from Genesis 12:6-7 "Abram passed through the country to the sanctuary of Shechem, the Terebinth-tree of Moreh […] there the Lord appeared." In the time of Joseph there was a giant terebinth tree near Hebron, legend states that it had been there since the creation of the world. I noted this legend down, but did not site it. It is connected to the works of Flavius Josephus, 37 C.E. Web.

Added Beauty: is inspired by research into the mythology of the peacock, who is likened to Christ because its flesh rots slowly. Also, by comments made by Charles Darwin in *Life and Letters of Charles Darwin*, vol. II, Francis Darwin, editor. New York: D. Appleton & Co.,1899.

...I remember well the time when the thought of the eye made me cold all over, but I have got over this stage of the complaint, and now small trifling particulars of structure often make me very uncomfortable. The sight of a feather in a peacock's tail, whenever I gaze at it, makes me sick! p. 90, a letter from C. Darwin to Asa Gray, 3 April 1860

...But I grieve to say that I cannot honestly go as far as you do about Design. I am conscious that I am in an utterly hopeless muddle. I cannot think that the world as we see it, is the result of chance; and yet I cannot look at each separate thing as the result of Design... Again, I say I am, and shall ever remain, in a hopeless muddle. Ibid., vol. II, p. 146, a letter to Asa Gray, 26 Nov. 1860.

Raven's Skein: the epigraph comes from Yeats' "Crazy Jane and Jack The Journeyman".

Song of Songs, III: En-gedi is the Hebrew for "The Spring of the Goat," a place name in the bible.

Storks, Eastern Europe: is set in Panariai in Lithuania just outside Vilnius. It is the place where hundreds of thousands of Jewish people were killed and buried in open pits.

The poem is inspired by photographs by Elizabeth Edelglass of storks on wires and by this quote and article: "The white stork is one of the most protected birds in the EU and Lithuania could get assistance to manage the problem of stork nests [on high voltage electricity pylons]," Laimutis Budrys, Environment Ministry. Terra. wire.com, 2005. Web.

The Crusades: the epigraph is from Shakespeare's *Julius Caesar.*

The Lord God Bird: is inspired by Phillip Hoose's *The Race to Save the Lord God Bird.* New York: Melanie Kroupa Books, Farrar Straus and Giroux, 2004. Many of the descriptions and the quotes were taken from this book. Part of the poem is set in the Linley Valley Cottle Lake Park, Nanaimo, BC.

Important References Also Include

The New English Bible, Illustrated by Horace Knowles. Oxford: Oxford University Press, 1961.

The New Oxford Annotated Bible 3rd Edition. Ed. by Marc Brettler, Z, Newsom, A. Carol and P. Perkins. Oxford: Oxford University Press, 1989.

J. Nicolai, D. Singer and K. Wothe. *Birds of Britain and Europe*, Trans and adapted by Ian Dawson. London: Collins Nature Guides, HarperCollins Publishers, 1993.

Alsop, Fred J. III, *Birds of North America: Western Region.* New York: DK Publishing Inc. 2001.

Google and Wikipedia for all manner of bird and bible facts, myths and stories. www.godweb.org/morebirds was invaluable in getting me started.

Acknowledgements

Poems here appeared in the following anthologies and journals, sometimes in different forms: *Force Field: 77 Contemporary BC Women Poets* and *Rocksalt: An Anthology of Contemporary BC Poetry* (Mother Tongue Publishing), *Babylon Burning: 9/11 Five Years On* (Nthposition.com), *Otherwheres: UEA Creative Writing Anthology 2005* (Pen & Inc Press), *Best Canadian Poetry in English, 2008* (Tightrope Books), *Descant, Grain*, www.connotationpress. com, www.poetsletter.com (UK), and www.branchmagazine.com. In addition poems under the title "The Genesis Birds" were shortlisted for the CBC Literary Awards. Many thanks to the editors of these presses and publications for supporting writers and poetry.

I am grateful for the support of the Canada Council for the Arts as well as the BC Arts Council for grants to work on poems in this collection and for assistance in attending Summer Literary Seminars in Lithuania. I'm also grateful for an International Scholarship from UEA.

At UEA I had the privilege of working with Denise Riley and George Szirtes. I'd like to thank both of them and my poetry cohort. Also thanks to the UEA Library and the Cambridge University Library for the many hours and the many many books. I'd also like to thank Jane and Wayne Thom for suggesting Ravenna, Italy and for sending me photographs, maps and details of where to go. To see the mosaics of birds and other animals there was a gift. I had a newborn son (now 8) and between my husband and parents we managed the baby and the research. My dad found the sculpture that inspired Abstine, so I thank him, my research assistant. Also, my sister-in-law Angela Stott ordered to her Pemberton Secondary School library the book *The Lord God Bird* by Phillip Hoose and so I found the Lord God Bird there. Thanks to the Waywords, my stalwart writing group for so much. Thanks to Wendy Morton, Rhonda Ganz, Ariel Gordon, Barbara Pelman and Cynthia Woodman Kerkham, readers and friends. Thanks also to the reading series Planet Earth Poetry in Victoria BC and all the poets I've met on Friday nights and to the gang at Café Writers in Norwich, UK. For his fine clear eye, I thank Carmine Starnino, and for giving these poems a home, I thank Dawn Kresan and Aimee Parent at Palimpsest Press.

Finally, thanks to my parents, Clive and Rita Blomer for being so amazing in every way. To Rupert Gadd who put his career on hold for a year so we could live in Norwich and for his love. Always love and thanks to my son, Colwyn, for opening my eyes daily.

Author photograph taken by Rupert Gadd

Author Biography

Yvonne Blomer lives in Victoria, BC where she works as a poet, memoirist, writing teacher, event organizer, and mom. She was born in Zimbabwe and came to Canada when she was two years old. Her poetry collections include *The Book of Places* (2012), and *in this moment the world* (2003),which was shortlisted for the Gerald Lampert Memorial Award. Yvonne has also published two chapbooks *Landscapes and Home: Ghazals* (2011) and *Bicycle Brand Journey* (2012), and is the co-editor of *Poems from Planet Earth* (2013) out of the Planet Earth Poetry reading series, of which she is the Artistic Director. Yvonne is currently working on a travel memoir titled *Sugar Ride* about cycling in Southeast Asia.

www.yvonneblomer.com.